Hidden Splendors of the Yucatan

Hidden Splendors of the Yucatan

Lalo Fiorelli

Editor: Lalo Fiorelli
Editorial Assistant: Katey O'Neill
Graphic design and production: Katey O'Neill
Published in Soquel, California
Printed and bound in Hong Kong through Bolton and Associates, San Rafael, California

Library of Congress Control Number: 2004093069

ISBN: 0-9717228-2-X
ISBN: 0-9717228-3-8

FRONT COVER: "OTHER WORLD." CUZEN AH PASSAGE, SAK AKTUN CAVE SYSTEM.
BACK COVER: "CATHEDRAL IN HEAVEN'S GATE." NOHOCH NAH CHICH CAVE SYSTEM.
HALF-TITLE PAGE: "BLUE REFLECTIONS," FROM UNDER THE SURFACE OF AN AIR BELL, NOHOCH NAH CHICH CAVE SYSTEM.
TITLE PAGE: "LACE EDGES." BACON-STRIP STALCTITES, MAYAN BLUE CAVE SYSTEM.

Contents

"The Torch" in the Sak Aktun cave system.

Preface

For most people, the opportunity to visit and explore an underground cave environment is a rare or impossible occurrence. Along with that, the underwater cave environment imposes a very difficult challenge. What exists in this fabulous world of darkness is an incredible variety of constant change. It has the artistic power of nature creating an array of unique shapes and sizes as if using the sweeping strokes of an artist's brush. From the minute and delicate soda straws and stalactites to the gigantic columns and flowstone, these speleothems have evolved during a meandering movement of geological time.

This spectacular pictorial book by Lalo Fiorelli captures breathtaking glimpses of this wonderful and pristine place. During the years of 1987 to 1994, Lalo and his spouse Evy were part of a very small but growing number of dedicated cave divers who discovered and began the first explorations and mapping of the cave systems located in the Akumal/Tulum area of Mexico's Caribbean coast. It began in 1985 with the exploration of the Carwash System. Soon after was the discovery and exploration of the Temple of Doom, Naranhal system (Mayan Blue and Naharon cenotes), Dos Ojos, Sak Aktun, Nohoch Nah Chich, and Calavera system. Each new discovery was an overwhelming experience, with an impressive variety and stunning volume of cave passages to explore and beauty to admire. Finding ancient human and animal skeletons, Mayan archeological artifacts, and new biological cave specimens was part of the dramatic evolution of this work that revealed an incredible new frontier. For those of us who were part of this historic and exciting period, it was a life-altering point in time and the best experience in an exciting era.

Lalo's contributions for safe cave diving included vital participation in the structural foundation of the National Association for Cave Diving's (NACD's) training standards and procedures. Lalo's photo image presentations at the NACD's annual seminars always gave vivid and exciting memories that would last a lifetime. His relentless pursuit of exploration in the Sak Aktun cave system located near Tulum helped document the data collecting and mapping that is kept and maintained in the files of the Quintana Roo Speleological Society. In addition, Lalo's photo documentation of key findings of ancient archaeological discoveries and new biological specimens helped science and the diving community be aware and informed of these important results.

Today, this area of the Yucatan has become known as the Riviera Maya. It is regarded as one of the world's most popular tourist destinations. Since 1985, in excess of one hundred cave systems have been discovered, explored, and surveyed. Nine of the top-ten longest underwater cave systems are located in the Riviera Maya. The longest, Ox Bel Ha, has more than 400,000 feet of explored and surveyed passageways.

Lalo's astonishing images have seized these precious diving moments and presented an opportunity for many people to experience and understand the spirit and adventure of this remarkable new world. *Hidden Splendors of the Yucatan* invites the reader to enjoy images of and learn more about this incredible and exciting frontier.

—Steve Gerrard

Editor's note: Steve Gerrard was president of the National Association for Cave Diving from 1985 to 1988. He is currently the Membership Committee Chairman, and an active cave diving instructor. He is responsible for considerably more cave diving certifications than anyone in the history of the NACD.

REFLECTIONS IN THE CAVERN ZONE, DOS OJOS CAVE.

Introduction

Flying south from the city of Cancun on the east coast of Mexico's Yucatan Peninsula, the view is spellbinding, with the Caribbean Sea to your left and the lush green jungle to your right. The scene brings forth all the emotions and fantasies one associates with exotic tropical locations and adventures. The jungle appears littered with diamonds, scores of them sparkling through breaks in the jungle canopy. Actually these diamonds are cenotes—natural limestone ponds—created when the roofs of underground rivers collapsed. Many of these cenotes are the entrances to caves with twisting, water-filled passages that run for miles through the soft limestone. There is virtually no above-ground fresh water on the peninsula, except where the roofs of these underground rivers or aquifers collapsed to create the cenotes. The entire peninsula is honeycombed with these caves.

Prior to the end of the last ice age, all of these Yucatan caves were dry and had features similar to what one finds in such famous dry caves as Carlsbad Caverns. During the end of the last ice age, about 10,000 to 13,000 years BP (Before Present), these caves flooded as sea levels around the globe began to rise. Gradual flooding is evidenced by water-level marks on the cave walls, indicating relatively long periods of stable water levels. Once completely flooded, all active cave formation processes were halted. Thus, we have a simple way to determine the age of the smallest of the limestone formations as being 10,000 to 13,000 years old, to coincide with the end of the last ice age. Huge, full-column speleothems (limestone drip formations) are tens of thousands of years old, but precise dating would, unfortunately, require destroying them for scientific study.

No man entered any of these Yucatan caves for at least 10,000 years, until the mid-1980s when a small group of United States explorers began to enter them with the aid of scuba. I joined this group during the first explorations. I worked in these caves as a cave diver and underwater photographer for eight years, from the beginning of 1987 through 1994. Exploration continues today, as the region—now known as the Riviera Maya—and cave diving have become more popular. New caves continue to be discovered, and links continue to be found between existing caves.

These caves exist within the Yucatan Mayan homeland, where the Mayan culture has been flourishing for centuries. The current Mayan culture carries with it many legends, superstitions, and myths from the past. One such superstition is a fear of the underground that is associated with their God Chac-mool. Chac is sometimes credited with responsibility for bad events. Because we ventured not only underwater, but also underground into the domain of Chac, the local Maya held us in high esteem.

One of the most interesting and persistent Mayan legends speaks of the existence of underground rivers on which it was possible for brave travelers to journey. It is said they went underground by boat between the great Mayan cities of Tulum, on the lower peninsula, and Chichen Itzá, to the northwest. In fact the general orientation of the caves is northwest to southeast. Evil spirits or not, there is geological evidence that such underground rivers may have really existed and been navigable.

When I gave a photo presentation to Marine Science students at the University of California, Santa Cruz, a student asked an interesting question. "How do we know these photographs are underwater?" I was stymied, and my only response was, "You have my word." A member of the San Francisco chapter of the National Speleological Society who was present asked if he could help answer the question. "It's easy," he said, "No footprints!" Water clarity in the caves is extraordinary. Visibility is in excess of 200 feet. Only diver movement and exhaust bubbles disturb this clarity. In the event of careless diving technique, the visibility can be reduced to zero in a matter of seconds.

A fact of life with underwater cave images is "scatter" that is caused when our lights illuminate suspended particles. When we are able to side light the scatter, this makes the smallest possible visible image of these particles (think of a half moon). Scatter is due to silt particles that come off cave ceilings and floors due to the disturbance caused by divers' bubbles and the wake of their passage. This is also the reason for the apparently odd leg position (knees bent up) of the divers in these photographs, as they try to minimize silting. Many of these images have unavoidable scatter in them. In some cases the scatter becomes an artistic element of the composition.

All the images were made underground, underwater, and in total darkness except for lights carried by the divers, except where noted otherwise in the captions. The obvious exceptions are images shot using natural light outside the cave or in the cavern entrance zone. The photo captions often include, in quotes, the descriptive or artistic name of a given cave formation or cave room; made at the time of our initial discoveries, these names came to be accepted by the diving community and were often used as locators during dives.

At the time we did this work, Mayan as a written language was still evolving, and written spellings were constantly changing. The phonetic spelling throughout this book is my own attempt to approximate the spoken language. There has been much work done to codify the written Mayan language, and today dictionaries exist that purport to be the "definitive" spelling; however, I ask the reader's indulgence with regard to the phonetic Mayan spelling used in this book.

I hope you are entertained and fascinated by the images and stories in *Hidden Splendors of the Yucatan*. The geology and anthropology is presented in a non-academic manner for the enjoyment of both the cave-diving community and the general public.

The long cavern zone, Nohoch Nah Chic cave.

FULL-COLUMN SPELEOTHEMS IN MAYAN BLUE CAVE, SHOWING THE COLOR THE CAVE IS FAMOUS FOR.

Diver Evy Cambridge in "Little Places," Sak Aktun cave.

Acknowledgements

For eight years (1987-1994), I made three or four 18-day trips annually to the Yucatan cave sites. During that time, I had several diving partners, including, for the last four years, my beloved spouse Evy Cambridge.

Some truly great "Speleonauts" did much of the early exploration of the cave systems. Among them were Steve Gerrard, Parker Turner, Jim Coke, Denny Atkinson, and Mike Madden. All of us who came during and after their efforts owe them our sincere gratitude for finding these fantastic caves and exploring their unknown reaches.

I would like to thank my original cave diving instructors, Jeff Bozanic and Steve Gerrard. They taught me the skills that allowed me to feel comfortable in the "dark" so I could concentrate on creating these images. Steve became my mentor and was my course director when I received my underwater cave diving instructor credentials from the National Association for Cave Diving (NACD). He was then the president of the NACD and is still an active instructor. He continues to work with me, and he was invaluable in helping on the preparation of this book.

I am grateful to all my dive partners for their knowledge, technical expertise, and camaraderie. Mike Madden taught me the caves and was my initial partner doing my remote lighting. Mike and I dove with Ron Winiker who is actually responsible for bringing an awareness of this wonderful alien environment to my attention. Ron and I were partners for our original cave diver certification course in Florida and during some of the Yucatan cave diving. Juan Jose Tucat, an oil field dive supervisor, was my next partner. He was like a machine underwater, and when diving with him, I always knew my back was covered. JJ, as he liked to be called, was actually a better diver than I. After the first two years, Evy Cambridge came on every trip, eventually becoming my best dive partner of all, and a very competent cave diver in her own right.

The first human remains of significance found in the Yucatan underwater caves were discovered by Buddy Quatelbaum. He came to me one night quite excited. He had made a primary exploration dive in a new cave and wanted Evy and me to dive the cave to photograph what he had found—the first human skull. Jim Coke made the most significant find—a full skeleton—while doing an exploration dive in the far reaches of the cave known as Mayan Blue. Without Jim's extraordinary talent as an explorer, this find would have been improbable. He led me there to photograph this full set of remains. Over several years, Jim and I became friends. He was the course director for my certification as a cave dive instructor with the National Speleological Society Cave Diving Section (NSSCDS).

Our work required a great deal of logistical support. Nancy and Tony DeRosa of Villas DeRosa were indispensable to our project. We lived in the downstairs of their duplex, and their dive operation provided all our tanks, vehicles, and porters. We grew to love them and their family as dear friends.

There were many people involved in these exploratory cave dives during the years I was there. If I have forgotten to acknowledge someone, I apologize.

"The Hobbits," below the halocline in the Temple of Doom cave.

Speleogenesis: Birth of a Limestone Cave

Throughout geological history there have been many great variations in climatic conditions that have caused the sea level to rise and fall by significant amounts. Sea floors are made of many layers of shell material. Over time and under pressure from water depth, these layers compress to form limestone (karst) rock. Almost the entire Yucatan Peninsula is old sea floor—karst rock. The caves formed at a time when the sea level was low and the karst rock was exposed to speleogenesis.

Water is the key element in the formation of a limestone cave. Rain picks up carbon dioxide as it falls and becomes mild carbonic acid. After reaching the earth, it percolates through the ground until it encounters an aquacline (non-permeable layer) through which it cannot pass. The water then travels along the aquacline. The mild carbonic acid puts the calcified layers into solution and in the process a cave is formed. This solution is calcium carbonate, the raw material of the decorations called speleothems.

Once the carved out passage is dry, the continual dripping of this solution into the cave forms the speleothems. Formations created from the ceiling downward are stalactites. Those that form on the floor of the cave and grow upward are stalagmites. When a stalactite and a stalagmite develop to the point of joining, they form a full column. This process of decoration can only occur when a cave is dry.

At the end of the last ice age, the sea level started to rise gradually and the Yucatan caves were completely flooded. As explained in the introduction, once they were flooded, the formation of their decorations was arrested. We know from water-level marks on the walls of the caves that this process was gradual. There had to be relatively long periods of water level stability to leave these marks, lines really, in the caves. It is only in the salt water below the halocline (the interface between the fresh water upper levels and the salt water below), that the mineral formations continue to change. The chemical action of the saltwater on the limestone erodes the formations, leaving shapes and forms that fire the imagination.

Sak Aktun

Sak Aktun ("White Earth" in Mayan), in the vicinity of Tulum, is arguably the most photogenic cave we dove in Yucatan. Because of its beauty, we dove in Sak 51 times during our eight-year project, photographing and exploring this almost pure white cave. The most memorable area of this cave complex is the Cuzen Ah passage. This is a circuit off the main line into a crystalline, delicate fairyland. The formations on the uphill side of this narrow passage actually sparkle in the beam of divers' lights.

Aktun is a very intimate cave, filled with several small passages and rooms. The smallest of the passages contain many major restrictions, which are places where divers must pass single file. As your partner carries your emergency air supply, the number and length of the major restrictions on any dive add tremendously to the technical difficulties of that dive. To negotiate these restrictions requires making moves that are more akin to rock climbing than to diving. The major difference, of course, is that the diver is neutrally buoyant in the water.

The most interesting campaign we did in Sak was accomplished in three dives, the first being in June of 1991, and finally accomplishing our goal of getting to the cenote known as Bosch Chen ("Black Well" in Mayan) in January of 1992. Here is an excerpt from my log of the first dive:

OPPOSITE: "ALADDIN'S LAMP."

LEE RACICOT AND AUTHOR EXITING CAVE AFTER AN EXPLORATION DIVE OF OVER A 5,000-FOOT PENETRATION. PHOTO BY EVY CAMBRIDGE.

Sak Aktun—The Maze
5 June, 1991
Diabolical! Fantastic! Evy and I went around the maze, as we had figured out how to do this on previous dives to a "T" at around 2,000-foot penetration. Turning basically south, we were led into an area of wonderfully difficult vertical major restrictions.

We got into downstream flow at around 2,500 feet and turned the dive at approximately 2,750 feet. This was diving with doubles and one extra single bottle. (This is called a stage bottle, and with two-thirds of its air supply remaining, it is shut off and left tied to the navigational guideline. It is retrieved on the way out of the cave, providing an adequate safety margin to our air supply.) *Due to recent storms around Tulum, the flow along the west main line and around the maze was too strong to allow us to quite complete this 3,000-foot traverse. At the point we turned the dive because of air constraints, we were at another area of major restrictions. I felt like I was on Bolam glacier on Mt. Shasta, that the difficulty of the passage warranted wisdom, not bravado. If the passage at this point had been bigger, we might have been tempted to go further. The opening monologue to Star Trek kept going through my head and wisdom called the dive.*

The best lesson we learned from diving in Sak has nothing to do with safety, or the mind-boggling grandeur of the cave, but rather concerns the art of relieving oneself while diving. This may not seem like a subject worthy of note, but the following anecdote shows that it can be very important for jungle cave divers.

Ever since infancy, we are trained not to urinate in our clothing. It is a hard habit to break; letting yourself "go" in a wet suit is difficult for this reason. The tendency is to hold it until you urgently need to relieve yourself, which generally occurs at the end of a dive, or during decompression. Usually this is not a big deal. Since Sak is a relatively shallow dive—50-foot schedule—dives with our doubles (double tanks) generally lasted about two hours and fifteen minutes, with a modest decompression schedule.

We had been diving in Sak for a few years, from a small cenote later named Ho Tul, before the Grand Cenote became available.

VIEW OF THE GRAND CENOTE FROM UNDERWATER IN THE CAVERN ZONE.

There were reports of bees nesting in the karst wall of the cenote. These bees started harassing divers, interestingly enough, usually at the end of the dive when exiting the water. We thought this was odd, since thus far we had not experienced any problem with them, although we knew they were present.

And now, for the fun: At the end of a particularly long dive with a four-person team, we were breaking down our equipment, kneeling in the water with the bees buzzing overhead. When we began to stand up, their furor was aroused. They were so agitated that we abandoned our gear and ran quickly toward the road, where they finally let up a bit. One of the team members had an old-fashioned wetsuit with a flap, called a beavertail, which connected through his legs. He had unfastened the beaver tail before the bees attacked, and while fleeing pulled the tail up over his head in an effort to get some protection from the bees. As he pulled up this piece of his wetsuit, the bees followed the tail of the wetsuit from his pelvic region to the top of his head. I saw all this and yelled to him to let go of the tail. We realized that what had set the bees off was the urine concentrated in our wetsuits.

So, the lesson learned was relieve yourself early and often during a cave dive in the jungle. This allows water to continually flush out the suit, and by the time you get out of the water, the bees won't bite your behind!

"POSEIDON" STANDS OVER TEN FEET HIGH, AND IS POSITIONED AT THE END OF CUZEN AH CIRCUIT.

"Other World" on the Cuzen Ah circuit, viewed across 30 feet of cave.

Caiman crocodile skull in the cavern zone of the Grand Cenote.

"Chac's Portal Into Night," an opening in the wall.

"ICE CREAM MELTS," A FLOWSTONE THAT IS PART OF A WALL.

"WINTER SNOW STORM," DIVER'S BUBBLES IN CUZEN AH PASSAGE.

"Little Buddha and Chopsticks" located in a small passage with many restrictions. Buddha is to the left rear in the image and stands only 15 inches tall.

"Hydra." This magnificent head is actually quite large, over four feet high.

Carwash

The discovery of what became known as the Carwash Cenote, also called Cristal (Spanish spelling) Cenote, marked the beginning of cave diving in this part of the world. Telling the story of this system is complicated by the fact that there are many versions of how and when it was discovered, and who did the first exploration dive. I will tell one version, and I wish to emphatically state that I do not want to take the glory away from anyone who thinks they deserve it.

As with many of the cave systems around the ancient pueblo of Tulum, this one is on the Coba road, a short distance from the main north-south highway. It is also closest to the road, thereby providing easy access. Mayans and Mexicans from the area had been using the cenote to wash their cars for years, which is obviously how the system got its name.

Sometime in the earlier part of the mid-1980s, Kumara Trowbridge, who was a U.S. dive store owner, led a dive group to Cozumel. One day they took the ferry from Cozumel to the mainland to make a few ocean dives and visit the Tulum and Coba ruins. On their way back from Coba, they saw the cenote from the road and decided to stop and rinse the salt water from their diving equipment with the fresh cenote water. While engaged in this pursuit, Kumara decided to jump into the cenote to cool off. He looked down and saw the darkness of the cave

"Cristal Cenote."

entrance. Using mask and fins, he made several free dives during which he saw some of the cavern zone formations and surmised there was a cave associated with them. While this is my story of the finding of this cave, Kumara was not cave-trained and did not make the first cave dive in this system. That part of the story gets so tangled that I will not make any attempt to tell it.

Opposite: Diver in "Room of Tears" at the end of the Madden Turner passage.

From a diver's standpoint, the logistics of diving this cave system are easy: park your vehicle next to the cenote, rig your equipment, and jump in. Because of its accessibility, Carwash was usually the cave we took new students to for their first cave dives.

The system contains both upstream and downstream passages, called the spring and siphon sides. In the spring side of a system, water flows from the ground. In the siphon side, water flows into the ground. These are accessed from opposite ends of the cenote. Approximately 600 feet into the siphon side is a room called the "Chamber of the Ancients." It was given this name due to what appears to be a fire pit cut into a free-standing limestone formation. There was burned charcoal found in the pit, presumably from the last fire burned here prior to the end of the last ice age when the cave was still dry. (See the section on Physical Anthropology, page 65, for images and further explanation.)

The siphon side of the cave also contains an area called "Satan's Silt Hole." This has suspended brown aqueous mud as a floor. It is extremely easy to stir up this mud and have visibility decrease from over 200 feet to literally not being able to see the beam from your light, in a matter of a few seconds (known as a silt-out). The reason for our repeated dives to this chamber with its very low ceiling and mud floor was to photograph *Typhliasina pearsi*, a variety of blind cave fish discovered in this area. They have no eyes but are extremely sensitive to vibration in the water, and approaching these wonderful creatures to photograph them was extraordinarily difficult. At times we had to abandon our objectives because we silted the area so badly in an attempt to swim beside the fish to photograph them in motion. Because of the possibility of such silt-outs, it was prudent to have one diver as a safety diver, responsible for maintaining contact with the navigational guideline and the diver doing the photography.

The main spring tunnel is unremarkable in color. However, further up the cave, and accessible only through the "Madden Turner Passage," is a magnificent pure white room. The passage is named in honor of Mike Madden and Parker Turner who discovered it and the "Room of Tears" beyond.

The first time Mike Madden led Ron Winiker and me into the "Room of Tears," we were overwhelmed with its beauty. This excerpt from my dive log explains our awe:

3 March, 1987
Cristal Cenote—spring side—"Room of Tears"

An absolutely magnificent dive! The single most beautiful place I have been on the planet, like being in the most beautiful cathedral ever! I could hear the organs playing. A penetration of about 1,100 feet total, past the "Chamber of Blocks" and the "Chamber of Horrors" into a very technical tunnel known as the "Madden Turner Passage." This passageway is roughly 150 feet long and begins after the "Curtain" and "Luke's Hope." The room is all white, very crystalline with many magnificent full columns. The ceiling is carpeted with soda straw stalactites. (Soda straw stalactites are much as the name implies—long, thin hollow formations, anywhere from four inches to over a foot long.)

Typhliasina pearsi: Views of two blind cave fish showing eye orbits—evidence that they evolved to this dark environment and once had eyes.

"The Thumb," part of a full-column formation in the Room of Tears.

Soda straw stalactites carpet the ceiling in the "Room of Tears," named for these delicate formations.

"Chamber of the Ancients." In this room on the siphon-side of the cave is the firepit with charcoal, which has been carbon-dated to almost 10,000 years ago.

Looking out from the cavern zone. The green color of the water is due to an algae bloom.

"The Curtain" is actually tree roots that have grown through the cave ceiling.

Mayan Blue

The cave known as Mayan Blue, although not easily accessible, offers many rewards. After a very bumpy ride on a track about two miles into the jungle, a single file-trail took us through areas where the jungle canopy closed in, making it impossible to see very far ahead. After a reasonably short walk, we came to a cenote. It was absolutely idyllic, with flowering vegetation, including bromeliads and orchids, around the perimeter. When we first came upon the cenote, we were at the entry point for a dive requiring about a 15-foot jump into the water. Looking down at the water from the edge of the cenote, we were amazed at both the color and clarity. The wonderful water color as seen from above was only a preview of the fantastic underwater blue palette caused by minerals in the water; these many shades of blue are evident in photographs from this cave system.

ABOVE, LEFT: MIKE MADDEN AND THE AUTHOR DOING A SURFACE DECOMPRESSION REST BEFORE EXITING THE WATER. PHOTO BY EVY CAMBRIDGE.
ABOVE, RIGHT: BROMELIADS FLOURISH ON THE RIM OF THE CENOTE.

When we first arrived in the Tulum area in early 1987, we were among very few cave divers there. At first we were well-received by the Mayans—they appreciated our respect for them and their culture, and they respected us for going underwater into the darkness of the caves. As time went by and the number of divers increased, some of the original good feelings wore off.

And then there was the cow! Well, actually not a living cow, but the whole carcass of a dead cow. The cow carcass became a symbol to us of the somewhat deteriorating relationship between the Mayans and the divers. The carcass was placed across the entrance to the trail leading from the dirt track where we left our vehicle to access Mayan Blue. Now I am not normally very squeamish, but think of what a dead cow left rotting in the sun and humidity looks like. Better yet, think of what it might smell like. We joked about breathing through our regulators until we were past this part of the trail. Several years later the bones were still present. No one ever tried to move the

THESE AMAZING STALACTITES ARE APPROXIMATELY 18 INCHES LONG. THIS IMAGE WAS PHOTOGRAPHED BY THE AUTHOR WHILE FLOATING ON HIS BACK, LOOKING UP AT THE CAVE CEILING.

carcass, and no one ever admitted to putting it there, nor why it was put there. It became sort of a guidepost to the trail entrance. We always wondered if we were being sent a message that we really were no longer very welcome, sort of like when the horse's head was put in the mafia Don's bed.

Cave systems seem to have predominant colors to their formations, based on the minerals in the ground water that created them, as well as substances in the water that coat or adhere to the surface of the formations. The Mayan Blue formations are a light sand color for the most part. However, when viewed through the water column while diving, almost everything in the cave appears to have been painted with a blue wash. Not surprisingly, that is how Mayan Blue got its name.

This cave system has both spring and siphon sides. It is in the siphon side that Jim Coke found our full skeleton, "Eckab." (Images from this skeleton are featured in the Physical Anthropology section, pages 74–75.) Eventually, the spring side was linked by a team of speleonauts to the siphon portion of the Naharon cave system.

Mayan Blue is a fairly easy cave to dive. The main passages are generally tall and contain no restrictions where divers would have to pass single file. It does have a few surprises in the off-shoot passages. An entry from my dive log tells the story of one such dive:

18 June, 1991
Mayan Blue—B-line

Evy and I went out the B-line to an arrow placed by Steve Gerrard indicating a place he had done some exploration. After making the six-foot jump to the right, (A jump is an unconnected gap between two guidelines that is left to avoid confusion while diving in the main cave. When a jump is made, a small reel is used to connect the gap for the duration of traversing that passage only, and is removed when exiting in reverse.) *we went out through a tall, narrow passage. This turns into a low—really low—flat, nasty tunnel no more than 2 feet high. With double tanks on our backs, we were only able to proceed with great caution. The reason we continued was we expected the cave to open up into a larger passage. It did not. We turned the dive in zero-visibility, and I was separated from Evy for over two minutes. The bottom is small, knobby limestone overlain with a couple of inches of muddy silt. Evy followed protocol and waited in a more clear area for me to appear. I was in contact with the navigational* (guide) *line and worked my way calmly back out of the passage. Evy later told me that she, while maintaining contact with the guideline herself, could feel the vibration I was creating on the line as I navigated in the zero-visibility back to her.* (One of the safety protocols of cave diving is that there be a continuous guideline laid from the cenote throughout the dive. In caves that are frequently dived, there is a guideline permanently installed in the main cave passages, as well as some of the offshoot passages.)

FULL-COLUMN SPELEOTHEMS—APPROXIMATELY 12 FEET HIGH—SHOWING THE COLOR THE CAVE IS FAMOUS FOR.

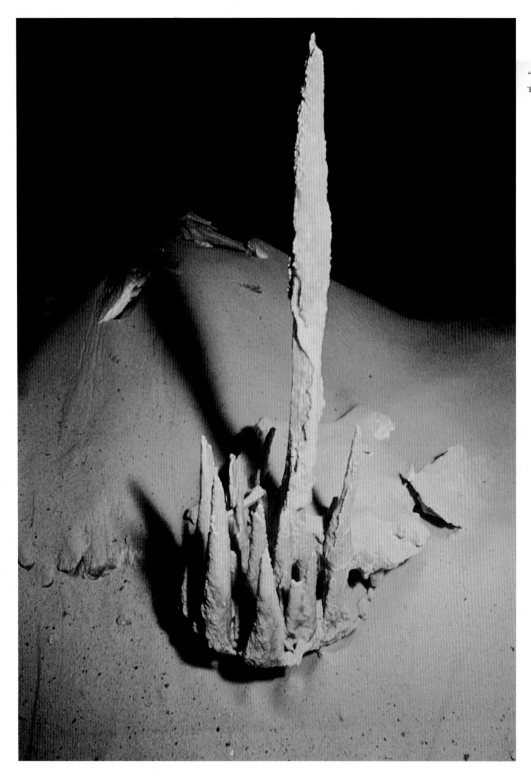

"DESERT MOSQUE" IS A PIECE THAT DROPPED FROM THE CEILING AND INVERTED AS IT FELL.

"Down the Hall" is a view of almost 60 feet of cave passage with an aqueous mud-silt floor.

These slender, graceful stalactites are over four feet long.

"LACE EDGES." DELICATE BACON-
STRIP STALACTITES WITH DARK RED
MINERAL STAINS.

Nohoch Nah Chich

The logistics of getting to some of the cave sites were difficult. Each diver's equipment, including double tanks, weighed approximately 110 pounds. Cameras, strobes, food, and drink also had to be carried into the jungle. All of the caves we dove are situated close enough to roads so that no overnight stays were required.

The physical discomfort of jungle travel was intense: the sweltering heat and humidity, the sweat running into our eyes, and the infinite variety of insects that plagued our every effort made each outing a challenge. The diving was so fantastic, however, that the misery was well worth it. As time went by, we did hire Mayan porters to carry the heavy equipment.

On Thanksgiving Day of 1987, divers discovered a new cave system for the first time: Nohoch Nah Chich, which means "Big Bird House" in Mayan. Nohoch added a new dimension to logistical problems. It is two kilometers into the jungle on an active Mayan ranch. Permission to dive the system was negotiated with the land holder. We had frequently hired Wilbur, a young Mayan man, as a porter. He kept telling us about a cenote on a ranch in the jungle. With Wilbur leading them, Mike Madden, Denny Atkinson, and Ron Winiker made the trip into the jungle, and the first dive of Nohoch occured on that Thanksgiving Day.

"Across Time and Space." A diver with a strong light in the back of this passage illuminates formations tens of thousands of years in-the-making.

We returned the following February to participate in the second dive team in this system. Between the first exploratory dives and our return, Mike had arranged for horses to carry our heavy equipment for the two-klick (kilometer) hike to the rancho. For ten days, we photographed and explored this magnificent cave. Each day, we loaded our equipment on the horses, hiked the

"The Dinner Plate." A beautiful bacon-strip stalactite being put on a "plate."

two klicks to the cenote, geared up, and made a dive usually over 100 minutes in elapsed time. Then we broke down the gear, loaded it back on the horses, and hiked the two klicks out. The spectacular dives were worth all the effort! We were diving and photographing in a truly virgin cave, a place never before entered underwater, and last visited by humans over 10,000 years ago when the cave system was dry.

Nohoch is another pure white cave. The main passages are huge and have grand rooms and galleries. A fantastic otherworldly display of nature's grandeur is arrayed along the sides of these tunnels. Formations of every description and size grace this very photogenic cave. As we swam through the passages, it was impossible not to see the formations as abstract representations. We named them for what they reminded us of, such as "Mr. Bill," "The Dinner Plate," "Heaven's Gate," and "The Torch."

Being a shallow system, averaging about 35 feet in depth, it was possible to make quite long dives on one set of double tanks. The cave begged to be photographed. As a result, it became common practice for me and my partner to carry two camera systems into the cave. We would shoot film in one area until our presence stirred up particles in the cave too much to continue, tie that camera off, and proceed up-cave to photograph in another place. On our return, we would retrieve the first camera and continue to shoot the previous location, which had cleared by then.

Through the efforts of Mike Madden and the men and women who dove with him on the Nohoch exploration projects for several years, Nohoch was added to the Guinness Book of World Records as the longest underwater cave in the world. At the time, it was a bit over 100,000 feet of surveyed passage in length. There was an ongoing rivalry between the divers of the Dos Ojos and Nohoch systems to maintain the length record,

and it has, by now, probably been back-and-forth several times. Nohoch is located on Rancho San Felipe, owned by Don Pedro Rodriquez Utizel and his family. Their home and fields are situated around the cenote that has served as their water well since long before divers discovered the cave. Rancho San Felipe is part of a group of land-grant ranches that are members of an "ejido," an agricultural co-op. When we first arrived, these people traded goods and services without much use of currency. They represented a vibrant indigenous culture, living on their native soil, and practicing a traditional subsistence economy. This is not to say they were poor. They had livestock, their corn cribs were full, and they had clean clothes. Their children were happy and well-cared-for, and the entire family appeared prosperous.

During our early visits to the rancho, the Señora had to walk the two kilometers out of the jungle to the paved road and hitchhike into Tulum to do her weekly shopping. As money became more of a factor in their lives, she would ride out on one of the horses Mike Madden bought them as part of the diving privilege agreement, and take a waiting cab on to town.

As the diving in Nohoch became more popular, Don Pedro received a fee for each diver who entered the system. This influx of cash actually created friction among the ejido members on whose jungle lands we traveled going to-and-from Nohoch. I continue to wrestle with the question of whether we did a good thing by introducing them to the concept of making money from their ranchos. It was sad to see how arguing over money gradually affected the joyful, happy community we first encountered.

"Cathedral in Heaven's Gate" is a small chamber within a huge partition wall that is 20 feet high, 20 feet long, and 6 feet thick.

REFLECTIONS FROM UNDER THE SURFACE OF AN AIR BELL.

"LEGACY OF THE WIND," A FOREST OF HELECTITES.

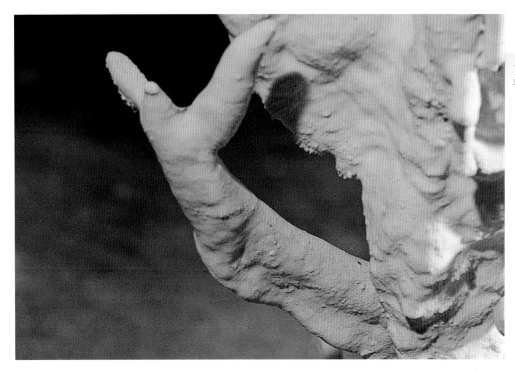

"Mr. Bill Climbs a Rock." A close-up of a helectite that is 6 inches tall.

"The Spur." Another close-up of a helectite.

"The Wedding Chapel" is part of a passage wall.

A LONG VIEW ACROSS A VIRGIN CAVE PASSAGE THAT IS QUITE WIDE BUT ONLY FIVE FEET HIGH.

Tanks being loaded on horses for the two-kilometer trek into the jungle.

Tanks being lowered by rope into the cenote-entrance area.

Wash day at the rancho. The "washing machine" is a hollowed-out log. Water is hauled by bucket from the cenote.

Naharon

Naharon is a very dark cave that seems to suck up the light. Due to the darkness of the walls and formations, being in this cave gives one a truly eerie feeling. The underlying color of the limestone is actually quite light, but everything is coated with a black substance which can easily be rubbed off with your hand. One of the prominent rooms in Naharon is Chac's Room, located about 1,500 feet from the entrance to the spring side of the cave. The Mayans associate the God Chac with spooky things, and in Naharon, particularly in Chac's Room, it is easy to imagine Chac lurking in the darkness.

While we were working in Chac's Room, my spouse Evy was having her own adventure. Evy, who was not my cave diving partner at the time, was waiting for us at the cenote entrance. This dive occurred at night, and as usual in this jungle, the bats came out to feed in the darkness. In their zeal to feed on the zillions of insects, the bats zoomed about Evy's head, unwittingly spooking her. We were gone on the dive for over two hours, including decompression time. When we finally surfaced around midnight, Evy was patiently waiting. Once she realized the bats were no real threat to her, the wait wasn't so bad, except for the biting, stinging insects.

In order to have enough air to remain on-station and do the photographing in Chac's Room, we dove with three scuba tanks

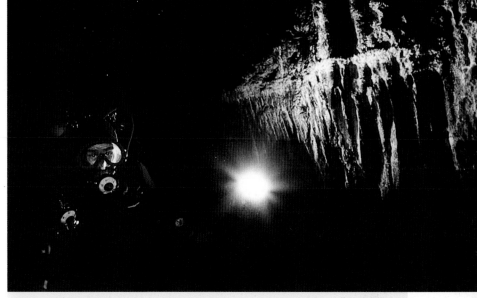

MIKE MADDEN'S DIVE LIGHT ILLUMINATES WATER-LEVEL MARKS ON THE CAVE WALL THAT GIVE CREDENCE TO THE MAYAN LEGEND OF TRAVEL BY BOAT UNDERGROUND BETWEEN CHICHEN ITZÁ AND TULUM.

each: one set of doubles on our backs and a stage bottle clipped in at our sides. This was not sport diving. With the depth involved and the amount of time spent underwater, we faced decompression schedules of over one hour.

Another significant passageway in Naharon is the Southwest Sacbe. The dive plan for this area was fairly complicated,

OPPOSITE: "FLIGHT THROUH INNER SPACE." A DIVER IN CHAC'S ROOM, 1,500 FEET INTO THE CAVE.

involving the use of three guideline reels as well as the permanent surveyed guideline. As in Chac's Room, in order to have the time on-station to do our work, we required three diving cylinders each in the Southwest Sacbe. The 60-foot passageway we photographed had red minerals on fairly light-colored stalactites, looking like blood dripping on teeth. In fact, these red colorations are called "Chac's Blood."

The dive area was difficult, involving a tall, narrow, nasty, silty passage within the halocline layer. It was impossible to stay above or below the halocline layer where visibility would have been dramatically improved. When approaching the halocline layer, the light shafts from our dive lights would bend as they hit it. Swimming through this layer stirs it up. If you are forced to stay in the layer, as we were, the visibility is as if grease were smeared on the lenses of your mask. Below the halocline, the

salt water tends to eat at the limestone, creating very delicate formations with a lot of loose particles on them. No matter how smoothly and slowly we moved about, we were forced to shoot the images in extremely poor visibility. This was due to loose particles from the formations being stirred into the water by our exhaust bubbles and our movements; this phenomenon is known as percolation.

Naharon also has a downstream, or siphon side. The siphon side of this very dark cave does not get dived much. However, it was used as the starting point to connect Naharon with Mayan Blue. Both are south of the city of Tulum: Naharon being on the west side of the main north-south highway, and Mayan Blue being on the east side. Mike Madden, one of the speleonauts who was involved in the exploration dive that made the connection, said that it was so nasty he never would do it again.

MIKE MADDEN REELING OUT OF THE CAVE, GIVING THE OK SIGNAL.

"Spooky Dark." Naharon is a dark, almost black, cave which seems to suck up light.

AUTHOR EXITING NAHARON CAVE. PHOTO BY EVY CAMBRIDGE.

Double tanks being carried through the jungle. Photo by Evy Cambridge.

"Chac's Blood," in the Southwest Sacbe.

A LARGER VIEW OF THE SOUTHWEST SACBE, ACROSS APPROXIMATELY 20 FEET OF CAVE. THIS PASSAGE
IS DOWNSTREAM AND BELOW THE HALOCLINE; VERY FINE GRAY SILT CAN BE SEEN ON THE CAVE FLOOR.

Balamcanche

Diving logistics for Balamcanche ("Hidden Altar" in Mayan) were quite interesting. Hillario Hiller got permission from the landowner and did the first exploratory dives of Balamcanche. With Hillario, we set out across a rough pasture carved out of the jungle, our route requiring passing several barbed-wire fences. We were introduced to this cave over five years into our work on the Yucatan, and by this time we were using strong, young Mayan men as porters. They carried the heaviest of our equipment, mainly our double dive cylinders, and we carried the cameras and remaining diving equipment. Without their help, we would have been exhausted by the time we were supposed to start the dive. Interestingly, though we had our shoulder harnesses on the tanks, they preferred to bear the weight of the tanks by forehead straps, as they bent over from the waist for leverage.

We reached the entrance to the cave at the end of a narrow path. It was a small hole, roughly eight feet in diameter at the top. After a short rappel down the almost vertical entry shaft, ducking under at the bottom, we arrived in a dry room with several openings to the sky. Tanks and equipment were lowered down the shaft with ropes. At one side of this room is a sump of very shallow water. As defined by the National Association for Cave Diving (NACD), a sump is "a water-filled section of an otherwise air-filled cave passage." NACD further states that

A POTTERY VESSEL AT THE EDGE OF A VERTICAL UNDERWATER CRACK; THIS VIEW MEETS THE DIVER UPON SURFACING WITHIN THE ALTAR ROOM.

sumps "tend to be located at places where the ceiling drops close to the floor." We started the dive via this sump. We placed our tanks on their backs in the water and then rigged our dive kits. We then lay down on our backs, wriggled into our harnesses, started breathing from our regulators, and then rolled over in the shallow, muddy pool. With a little more squirming, we

OPPOSITE: DIVER ON THE SURFACE, IN AN AIR BELL; THE HALOCLINE IS VISIBLE AT THE SURFACE-LEVEL OF THE WATER.

BALAMCANCHE   47

made our way to deeper water where we could start our descent under the far wall of the dry room and sump.

This cave system has a halocline at about 35 feet of depth. Consequently much of it is in salt water and is extremely fragile. Due in part to not having been previously dived, the percolation was pretty intense. Percolation is usually composed of very small particles that tend to stay suspended in the water column for quite a while. This cave was so fragile, however, that flat pieces as big as ten inches across formed part of the "rain." It was a little disconcerting when such large pieces hit you in the head while falling from the ceiling.

Above a knife-edge shelf in the halocline, we were greeted by an interesting phenomenon. There was an approximately ten-inch hole in the wall. Less than a foot out from the hole was a basketball-sized sphere of swirling water. We had found a "spring run" for this cave; fresh water was entering the cave from above. The mixing of the fresh water as it flowed into the saltwater below the halocline caused the "ball."

On our way back to the entry, only a short way into the cave, our guide Hillario motioned for us to ascend a narrow crack through which diffuse daylight filtered down to us underwater. We were soon to learn why this system was named Balamcanche, or Hidden Altar. After surfacing, we looked upon a site few had seen since classical Mayan times. The room was a shrine. In the middle was an old stalagmite that had been carved out, with slots on four sides. The ceiling of the room to our left was blackened with the soot of fires burned long ago, at an altar we couldn't quite see from our vantage point. Stairs carved into one wall originally led to the surface when the shrine was in use, but this stairway entrance was now blocked. The natural light filtering into the room came from a hole about four feet wide containing a lot of plant growth that impeded access by

A FOSSILIZED CONCH SHELL EMBEDDED IN THE CEILING OF THE CAVE.

the stairway. This daylight hole was about 20 feet above the floor of the room. Directly in front of me on a ledge was part of a small, earthenware pedestal bowl; a side piece had broken away. What a joy to be in a holy place for the ancient Maya, untouched by modern man!

New stalactites being formed in an air bell, showing water droplets on the ends of the small formations. A partial collapse of the cave ceiling, in this previously completely flooded cave, created an air bell allowing cave renewal processes to commence again.

Ponderosa

The Ponderosa cave system was discovered and first explored by my good friends Tony and Nancy DeRosa. Their wry sense of humor is responsible for the cave name. As a cenote is a pond in the jungle, and their name is DeRosa, the cave became known as Ponderosa. This was the name of the ranch portrayed in the old TV Western series, "Bonanza." Names used in the cave were derived from that TV series. Hence as one travels up-cave, you proceed from the Ponderosa to the Corral, then out Hoss's line to the Pool Hall, and up into the Chapel within the Pool Hall (think of Old West weddings performed using a pool hall for a chapel).

The Corral is a half-moon-shaped cenote reached by a short swim through a huge underwater tunnel big enough to drive a freight train through. The continuous guideline is tied off at regular intervals as it makes its way around the breakdown pile that formed the cenote. (A breakdown pile is the result of a roof collapse of an underground aquifer that exposes the aquifer to daylight, thus creating a cenote. It is also possible to have a roof collapse that doesn't open the aquifer to the daylight. In this case it is common to find an underground air bell.) The continuous guideline is reminiscent of the wood-railed fencing of the corrals on the namesake TV series. Natural sunlight filtering through the plants above creates beams of intense, neon-green light shafts in the water column. In the mud and leaf litter of

A DIVER FLOATS ON THE SURFACE UNDER STALACTITES IN THE POOL HALL, APPROXIMATELY 1,500 FEET INTO THE CAVE.

very shallow portions of this cenote, we found evidence of human habitation. By fanning the mud with our hands, we uncovered quite a few undecorated pottery shards. It was impossible to tell whether these were modern or antique, as Mayan people have continuously populated this geographic area since the Classical Mayan period.

OPPOSITE: A DIVER TRAVERSING THE CORRAL CENOTE ON THE WAY UP THE CAVE.

The Ponderosa cave system is shallow. Due to its close proximity to the ocean, north of Puerto Aventuras, the halocline is quite shallow, and much of the cave is in salt water. It abounds with air bells, which are rooms where one can surface in an air pocket. Before breathing the air in these places, we would check our depth gauges; a "0" told us the air pocket was at sea level. The presence of bugs and bats was another clue about air quality. Both these factors indicated an exchange of air from outside the bell. If these factors were not present, or if the air smelled bad, we would breathe through our regulators while in the air bells.

The Pool Hall is a huge breakdown room approximately 3,000 feet back in the cave. (A breakdown room contains an accumulation of collapsed ceiling material, but no hole open to the sky to create a cenote.) After surfacing in the air bell that is part of the Pool Hall, you enter the Chapel, a truly marvelous place. As previously explained, all the stalactites and stalagmites in the subaquatic portions of the caves were formed prior to the end of the last ice age, when the caves were dry. In the Pool Hall

there are thousands of living stalactites—new, growing cave formations representing the geological cycle in the process of renewal. Calcium-rich water droplets gleamed as our lights illuminated the spiky ends of the young stalactites. Many of the images of this system were photographed above water in the Pool Hall.

It was a delight to float on our backs on the water surface in the Chapel, viewing the multitude of stalactites pointing down towards us. The site of these large and somewhat ominous-looking formations reminded us of booby traps imbedded with spikes, as in the Indiana Jones movies that were popular during our work there. In fact, many of us in the cave-diving community joked about feeling as if we were in an Indiana Jones movie as we did these cave explorations. To add to the mysterious aspect of the Chapel room, our lights cast a green glow through the surface of the water, like looking through a piece of thick glass on edge. This refraction gave a wonderful quality to the light captured by our cameras.

FLOATING WHILE VIEWING THESE SPECTACULAR FORMATIONS
OFTEN GIVES THE DIVER A SENSATION OF BEING DISEMBODIED.

Nancy DeRosa in the Chapel of the Pool Hall.

NANCY DEROSA UNDER ACTIVELY FORM-
ING STLACTITES IN THE POOL HALL.

Sᴜɴ sᴛʀᴇᴀᴍs ᴛʜʀᴏᴜɢʜ ᴘʟᴀɴᴛs ᴀɴᴅ ʀᴏᴏᴛs ɪɴ ᴛʜᴇ Cᴏʀʀᴀʟ Cᴇɴᴏᴛᴇ.

Temple of Doom

The Temple of Doom cave system is about 300 to 400 meters into the jungle, and a very tough campaign. When we first dove the Temple, we would suit up at our vehicle, and wearing our wetsuits, walk to the cenote on a narrow trail in hot humid conditions. We then geared up and made the approximately 15-foot jump into the cenote. After a dive, the equipment was hauled out of the cenote on ropes, and we had to climb out using tree roots and vines, all this in the presence of an unbelievable number of biting insects. This system has my personal vote as the cave with the most bugs!

Our first view of the Temple of Doom cenote as it appeared through the jungle was astonishing because of the lush surrounding vegetation and the depth to the water surface. Our first dive here presented us with a new and unique challenge—bat guano! The cenote was created when the limestone roof of the underground aquifer collapsed. The rim of the cenote is roughly circular and well above the water surface, which was covered with a thin film. Once in the water and before beginning our dive, we could see thousands of bats hanging upside down on the underside of the cenote rim. It slowly dawned on us that we were immersed in the bat guano that was floating on the surface. After this first experience, I was careful to keep a regulator in my mouth as much as possible while on the surface to avoid accidentally ingesting any contaminated surface water.

DIVERS IN THE HALL OF GIANTS WITH THEIR BODIES HALF-ABOVE AND HALF-BELOW THE HALOCLINE.

The Temple of Doom has what is probably the largest single underwater room of the caves featured in this book. The "Hall of Giants," as the name implies, is huge. From the middle of the room, our light beams did not reach the far walls. In the center is a giant stalactite approximately three stories tall, from ceiling to tip, which grew to this size before the cave flooded from

"DRAGON HEAD AND STAR." AN ERODED LIMESTONE SCULPTURE BELOW THE HALOCLINE.

rising sea levels after the last ice age. The tip of the "Devil's Fang," as this mid-cave stalactite is called, is over ten feet from the cave floor. In the hall there is a halocline layer that is evident in photographs when divers intentionally place half of their bodies above the halocline, and half below. Underwater, much of the Temple is below the halocline, in salt water. The chemical action of the salt water and the subsequent erosion shapes the limestone into an array of forms that easily suggest known objects. Many of the cave formations were named according to the above-water objects they most resembled. Actually, while recognizable, these representative formations are eroded enough to look a bit like Swiss cheese. The originally hard limestone formations in the upper freshwater areas of the cave become soft and very fragile after interaction with the underlying salt water.

The Temple of Doom cave system was named after the popular movie "Indiana Jones and the Temple of Doom." That movie's sets could easily have been modeled from this cave system. The bizarre and eroded cave formations, the bats on the ceiling of the cenote, the bat guano in the water, and the verdant jungle location compare to scenes in the movie and led to the cave's name. What we saw as we conducted dive operations there gave us the same feelings we had watching that great movie. The name "Temple of Doom" conjures up images of underground caverns with booby traps and adventurous exploration. Unlike the protagonist in the movie, however, we gained no valuable treasure, nor was there anyone trying to kill us, but we were always aware of the potential dangers of the underground, underwater environment of this and all the caves we dove in.

THE RIM OF THE CENOTE OF THE TEMPLE OF DOOM CAVE SYSTEM.

"Cliff Dwellings." This formation was named for its likeness to a table-top model one might see in a museum devoted to the Indian cliff dwellings of the western United States.

"Mayan Totems" are full columns approximately eight feet high.

"Columns in the Sand" are formations located in Virgin Cave. When these photographs were taken, the floor of this cave had not been touched by humans since before the end of the last ice age.

A DIVER SWIMS THE CAVE. THE GRACEFUL LEG POSITION, WITH THE KNEES BENT UP, REDUCES THE EFFECT OF THE DOWN-WASH OF THE FINS AT THE BOTTOM OF A KICK, THEREBY MINIMIZING CLOUDING OF THE WATER BY PARTICULATE MATTER.

"Alpine City." This amazing formation was created by the limestone erosion from the salt water, below the halocline, leaving a sculpture looking much like a town amidst pine trees, covered with snow.

Physical Anthropology

The theory that the entire Americas was populated from north to south only by people migrating over the Asian land bridge seems to be a very simplistic explanation. This is, however, the mainstream view of academia. A growing body of evidence based on the findings of human remains suggests there were other sources of population of the Americas, perhaps by people who came by ship. The finds we made in the Yucatan caves challenge the mainstream view.

Those humans who came across the land bridge had skull features of Asian people, with skulls being wider across the forehead than they are from front to back (brachycephalic). This is the shape found in skulls from remains throughout the Mesoamerican timeline. This skull shape is also found among indigenous populations throughout the Americas today.

The exhibits at the National Museum of Anthropology in Mexico City are displayed in halls arranged by cultures from various times throughout Mexico's history. Among those included are the Mayans, the Aztecs, and the Toltecs. There is another exhibit hall called "The Other People" where human remains that are 5,000 to 10,000 years old are displayed. These bones have been placed in dioramas that depict how they were found in situ. There is little written explanation of these remains and the culture they came from. The skulls in this exhibit are longer from front to

A VERY OLD LONG BONE, PERHAPS A FEMUR, EMBEDDED IN THE CAVE FLOOR, IN AN AREA KNOWN AS "THE DRAIN," IN THE DOS OJOS CAVE SYSTEM.

back than they are wide across the forehead (dolichocephalic), and this shape is mainly Caucasoid or Negroid in origin.

When I speak of the Mesoamerican timeline, I am specifically referring to the emergence of Indian cultures in Mexico. Although sources vary somewhat, the beginning of the timeline

OPPOSITE: THE FIRST HUMAN SKULL DISCOVERED IN THESE SUBAQUATIC CAVES BY BUDDY QUATELBAUM. THE ENTIRE CAVE SYSTEM WAS NAMED "CALAVERA" (SKULL) IN HONOR OF THIS DISCOVERY. THE IMAGE CLEARLY SHOWS THE CRANIAL SUTURES.

(Pre-Classical period) is generally accepted as being between 1500 and 1800 BC. The commonly held theory is that there are no indigenous Mesoamerican human remains from before this time. The great significance of the finds made in the Yucatan submarine caves is that they present evidence of earlier human presence and the possibility of access routes other than the Asian land bridge. The skulls found in the caves are dolichocephalic, exhibiting the Caucasoid/Negroid shape, which supports the concept of an alternate migration route.

One of our earliest finds was a fire pit in the siphon side (water flows into the ground on the siphon side of a submarine cave) of the Carwash Cenote in a room known as the Chamber of Ancients. This structure is an inverted cone of natural limestone, with a pit dug into it and two vents out the sides. The charcoal and burnt sticks are evidence of use. We did not wish to disturb the actual arrangement of the charcoal in the pit, but collected a few samples lying on adjacent rock. The carbon in these samples was dated to 9600 years BP (Before Present). The carbon dating of this fire pit proves that there were humans on the Yucatan Peninsula predating the commonly held ideas of the start of the Mesoamerican timeline.

The caves themselves offer help in establishing a rough age for the remains. As mentioned in the introduction, we know these caves have not been dry since the end of the last ice age, approximately 10,000 to 13,000 years ago. According to accepted anthropology theories, there were no humans on the Yucatan Peninsula prior to the Asian land bridge that was exposed during the last ice age. The Yucatan caves flooded after the end of that ice age. Any Caucasoid/Negroid remains in those caves had to have walked into the caves when they were dry (during the last ice age). Human remains in these caves can therefore be dated to the last dry era, or at least 10,000 years ago. There was no use of these caves by the Mayans or any other Mesoamerican cultures, as they were not present when the caves were dry.

The human remains found in these underground, underwater cave systems are not to be confused with skeletal evidence of centuries-old Mayan sacrificial victims thrown into open cenotes. Their age, skull shape, remote location, and association with the fire pit all tell a different and more ancient story. As our diving community continued to explore the caves, other finds were made which support the age of the remains. The first bones were found in the Carwash. They are at the bottom of a ten-foot-deep shaft in the Hall of Blocks. They appear to be leg and arm bones and are folded into what looks like a fetal position. In an attempt to photograph them, I was lowered into this shaft head-first with someone holding my feet. I got the photos, but because of the tight confines of the shaft, a cloud of particles from the walls obscures a clear view of the bones. Since the shaft is so narrow and deep, we never returned for fear of completely covering the bones.

A few years later a cave diving explorer friend of mine, Buddy Quatelbaum, approached me about a find he had made. He was reluctant to tell me exactly what it was, but knew I was interested in old human remains. We dove the new cave with him the following day, and what he had found was the first human skull. To commemorate the occasion, I named the cenote Calavera (skull) cenote. This was a very exciting find, especially as this skull exhibited the dolichocephalic characteristics of Caucasoid/Negroid remains.

Later in the same year Buddy came to tell us of yet another find. He was exploring the cave called Dos Ojos (Two Eyes), which has two cenotes connected by an underwater passage—both cenotes leading into the cave. The floor of the passage is sandy and drops away as you enter it, diving from one cenote to the

The fire pit on the siphon-side of the Carwash Cenote cave system. Evidence of the sticks of wood that made this fire are apparent. A small sample of the charcoal, taken from the floor around the pit, was carbon-dated (C14 method) at 9,600 BP (Before Present).

other. This area had become a drain, working much like the U-shaped trap under a sink. Over who-knows-how-much-time, many animal and human bones ended up here. Among the most significant is a human jawbone with several molars still in place, and a long bone that could be a femur. Buddy guided us to this site, and we photographed these remains.

Buddy also took us on a cave dive to show us what looked like a burial mound. The mound had a light shaft shining on it from a five-foot hole in the cave roof high above it. The mound was made from solid pieces of undecorated limestone two to three feet wide, which definitely did not come from inside the cave. The shaft of light directly above the top of the conical shape made for an eerie sight, as if a searchlight was intentionally shining on the mound. We knew again not to disturb the mound; to do so would invalidate any future scientific work. We did, however, fan the floor of the cave right next to the mound, and were rewarded with the find of two human teeth. I moved one of them to a black background where I was able to photograph it, and then returned the tooth to its original location.

Images of this tooth were later sent to Professor Donald Morris at Arizona State University whose specialty is forensic odontology (the anthropological study of teeth). Along with the images, Dr. Morris received a copy of the C14 (carbon) dating documentation from the charcoal in the fire pit at the Carwash. He and two of his colleagues studied the images and reported that the enamel of the tooth, the four cusps, and the "pinhole" (cusps not fully developed as in modern teeth) are all common features in early Native Americans.

I asked Dr. Morris about the wear on the cusps and whether it was from diet or tooth-to-tooth contact. His reply was that since they determined the tooth was from a young person, the excessive wear was most likely due to diet. Prehistoric tooth samples, he said, often exhibit wear due to diet in young individuals, and such wear helps establish that the tooth is old. Grinding of corn two thousand or more years ago left much grit in the meal and produced a coarser grind than that found in modern corn meal and masa (corn dough). Dr. Morris concluded that "if the tooth in the photographs is from the cenote, and if it is 10,000 years old, in my opinion no extraordinary explanation is necessary to account for it."

Early in the next year I was approached about the finding of a full skeleton, what came to be the "crown jewel" of all our discoveries. Jim Coke, one of the premier underwater cave explorers in the area, made the find while doing a big dive in the downstream section of the cave known as Mayan Blue. Jim named the skeleton Ekcab. This metaphysical name loosely means Star in Heaven in Mayan. He graciously led me to his find to photograph it. The dive required carrying an extra tank besides our double tanks because it involved a fairly long penetration. Ekcab's skull exhibited the dolichocephalic characteristics of Caucasoid/Negroid remains, implying it was over 10,000 years old.

Having accumulated all this physical evidence we decided to approach INAH (National Institute of Anthropology and History) of the Mexican government, which we did through the American Embassy in Mexico City. Lee Racicot, my partner in this venture, and I made a presentation of our finds to the then-director of archaeology for INAH. Our efforts were rewarded, and their initial interest was very high. We were involved with INAH for almost a year doing all the preparatory work for conducting dive operations aimed at recovering the remains and opening the burial mound. This was at the time of a change in government in Mexico, and eventually the door closed in our faces. Disheartened by this turn of events, we abandoned our attempt to bring this evidence to the academic community.

"CHAC APPEARS." A DIVER EMERGES FROM BEHIND THE CONICAL LIMESTONE FORMATION THAT CONTAINS THE FIRE PIT.

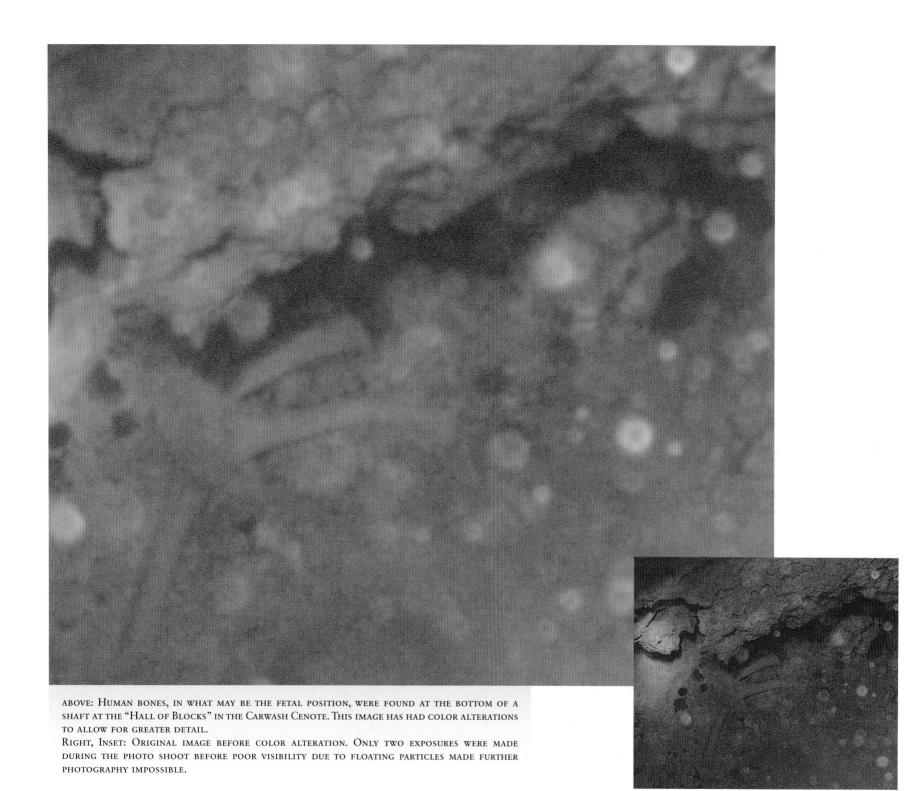

ABOVE: HUMAN BONES, IN WHAT MAY BE THE FETAL POSITION, WERE FOUND AT THE BOTTOM OF A SHAFT AT THE "HALL OF BLOCKS" IN THE CARWASH CENOTE. THIS IMAGE HAS HAD COLOR ALTERATIONS TO ALLOW FOR GREATER DETAIL.

RIGHT, INSET: ORIGINAL IMAGE BEFORE COLOR ALTERATION. ONLY TWO EXPOSURES WERE MADE DURING THE PHOTO SHOOT BEFORE POOR VISIBILITY DUE TO FLOATING PARTICLES MADE FURTHER PHOTOGRAPHY IMPOSSIBLE.

Another view of the first human skull discovered in the Calavera cave system. The debris field around it is clearly visible and contains many bone fragments. No other part of the skeleton was ever found.

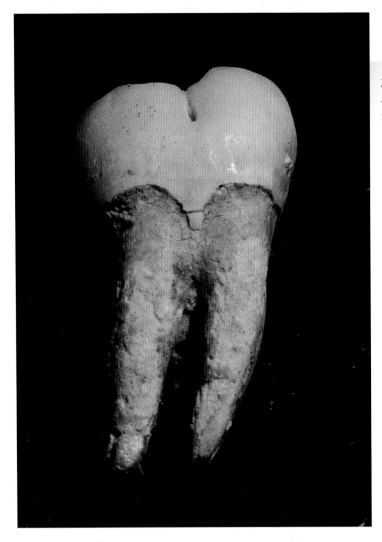

A MOLAR FOUND AT THE BURIAL MOUND IN THE TIC TE HA CAVE SYSTEM. THE PINHOLE NEAR THE TOP WHERE THE CUSPS JOIN IS EASILY SEEN, A FEATURE INDICATING EARLY INDIGENOUS ORIGIN.

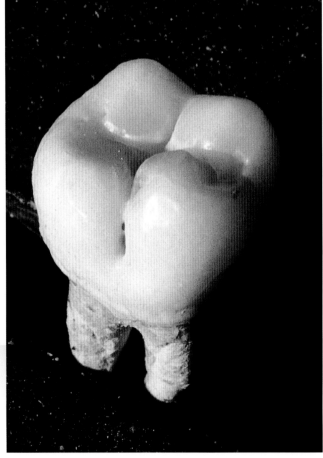

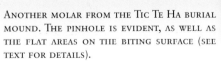

ANOTHER MOLAR FROM THE TIC TE HA BURIAL MOUND. THE PINHOLE IS EVIDENT, AS WELL AS THE FLAT AREAS ON THE BITING SURFACE (SEE TEXT FOR DETAILS).

A HUMAN JAWBONE WITH THE REMAINS OF TWO TEETH, FROM THE DRAIN IN THE DOS OJOS CAVE SYSTEM.

"Ekcab." the crown jewel of all the human remains from the Tulum area and the first full skeleton discovered. Ekcab was discovered in downstream Mayan Blue during an exploration dive by Jim Coke.

THE SKULL AND UPPER BODY SKELETON ARE REPRESENTED. IT IS CLEAR THAT THE SKULL IS LONGER THAN WIDE, AND THEREFORE NOT FROM A TRADITIONAL MESOAMERICAN INDIAN.

THE LOWER BODY SKELETON: PELVIS, RIBS, AND LEG BONES PARTIALLY COVERED WITH SILT.

Tulum Ruins: Temple of the Sun

TEMPLE OF THE SUN.

Tulum Ruins: Observatory

Astronomical observatory as seen from atop the Temple of the Sun,
looking north along the Caribbean coast.

"Frozen in Time." A small, elegant sculpture in Little Places, Sak Aktun cave system.

The Photography

All pictures of speleothems in this book were photographed underground, underwater, and in total darkness except for the lights we carried. The photographs are not the result of just a single attempt to capture the subject in each image. Developing the techniques for making artistic images in the darkness of a submarine cave required a review process. We would check transparencies, decide what techniques might improve the images, and return, sometimes several times, to photograph the same subjects again. In some instances we repeated the same dive plan to photograph the same subject three or four times.

When we started the project, we had no idea of what it was going to take to make quality images. Our initial efforts were with the strobes mounted at the camera. The results were pleasing, but very one dimensional. As our lighting techniques evolved, we developed a procedure using two divers, one to do the photography and one to do the lighting. The technique involves the placement of one or more strobes well off the plane of the camera —as much as 15 to 30 feet—as well as one or two strobes at the camera. This gives the photographs their three-dimensional effect.

Finding the best strobe location and direction to point the strobe heads was the most time-consuming aspect. Percolation, a phenomenon unique to this environment, was another photographic challenge. Because these caves were "virgin" when we did this work (no divers before us), there were many particles sticking to the cave ceilings. They became dislodged by our exhaust bubbles and "rained" on our setups. Consequently, after setting up to shoot, we had to clear the area and allow the percolation to settle. Then we swam into place, shot a few frames, and moved

away again. In some instances it took as long as 45 minutes to complete 14 frames of one composition, changing the lighting setups after three or four bracketed frames were shot for each.

As light travels through the water column, it loses the red-orange components of its spectrum almost completely by the time it has traveled 30 feet from the light source. Due to this fact and the unbelievable clarity of the water (visibility in excess of 200 feet), some images have a green color cast. Open water divers experience a blue-green world when diving below 30 feet without artificial light. Our strobes were the light source while diving in the otherwise total darkness of the Yucatan caves. In our most ambitious setups, the water clarity allowed us to shoot across 40 to 60 feet of cave. I believe that it is my obligation as a natural history photographer to present images as close as possible to what my mind's eye remembers seeing. Therefore, no effort has been made to correct the green cast in the photographs. The images are an accurate reflection of what we saw when diving.

All exposures were made on professional Kodachrome 200. Kodachrome was the only film at the time that had a high red-orange saturation. This helped keep the green cast to a minimum. All the Ektachrome, or E6, process films of the period tended to make terrestrial photographs suffer from a blue-green enhancement. In the total darkness of the underwater cave environment, the results of using E6 were unacceptable.

The cameras used were two Nikonos 5s with 15mm and 28mm lenses, and an F-3 Nikon with a 105mm macro lense in a housing. Several different size strobes, all Nikon, were used for the lighting.

Stop signs such as this have been placed by the National Association for Cave Diving (NACD) at the water-entry zone of the caves to discourage untrained divers from proceeding further. This one is in the Carwash Cenote. Photo by Steve Gerrard.

Safety in Cave Diving

Diving in underwater caves is an extremely hazardous activity. Specialty training is required that deals with equipment and techniques for this unique diving environment. Many untrained divers have died in caves, including open water scuba instructors. Three-foot-wide danger signs, like the one on the facing page, are placed inside cave mouths to discourage untrained divers from entering.

Cave diving is not sport diving! The cave diver enters realms for which no sport divers are trained. Cave diving is done in an overhead environment and frequently has multi-levels of decompression. In the open water, there is always an escape hatch—an ascent to the surface is always possible. But during a cave dive, all problems must be solved underground and underwater.

Almost all the regularly dived caves in the United States and on the Yucatan Peninsula have STOP signs. These signs are placed by members of the National Association for Cave Diving (NACD) and the National Speleological Society Cave Diving Section (NSSCDS). Members of these groups volunteer their time and effort to place these signs in the interest of public safety.

Cave diving courses usually run about a week, in which time students do approximately 13 dives and log around 20 hours of bottom time. The two primary organizations in the United States that provide this training are:

The National Association for Cave Diving [NACD]
P.O. Box 14492
Gainesville, Florida 32604
On the web: www.safecavediving.com

The National Speleological Society Cave Diving Section [NSSCDS]
2109 W. US Highway 90, Suite 317
Lake City, Florida 32055
On the web: www.nsscds.com

Spelean Philosophy

Take Only Pictures

Leave Only Bubbles

Kill Nothing But Time